This planner belongs to:

_____

_____

_____

 Thank yo so much for choosing our planners!
Your voice really matters,
so please don't hesitate to leave us a rating or review.

massy
planners

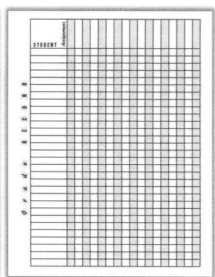

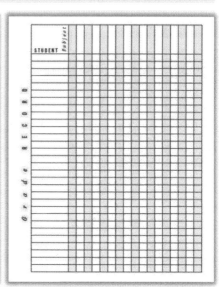

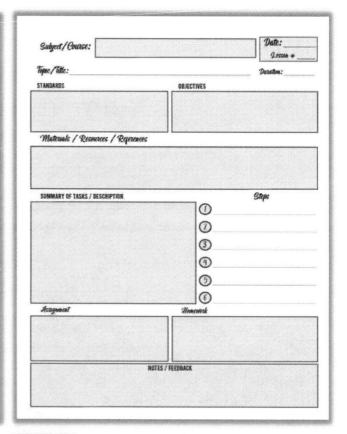

Scan the code:

Or use this link:

https://bit.ly/3aLhiev

livin' that TEACHER life

2022-2023 ACADEMIC YEAR

JULY

S	M	T	W	T	F	S
					1	2
3	4	5	6	7	8	9
10	11	12	13	14	15	16
17	18	19	20	21	22	23
24	25	26	27	28	29	30
31						

August

S	M	T	W	T	F	S
	1	2	3	4	5	6
7	8	9	10	11	12	13
14	15	16	17	18	19	20
21	22	23	24	25	26	27
28	29	30	31			

SEPTEMBER

S	M	T	W	T	F	S
				1	2	3
4	5	6	7	8	9	10
11	12	13	14	15	16	17
18	19	20	21	22	23	24
25	26	27	28	29	30	

October

S	M	T	W	T	F	S
						1
2	3	4	5	6	7	8
9	10	11	12	13	14	15
16	17	18	19	20	21	22
23	24	25	26	27	28	29
30	31					

NOVEMBER

S	M	T	W	T	F	S
		1	2	3	4	5
6	7	8	9	10	11	12
13	14	15	16	17	18	19
20	21	22	23	24	25	26
27	28	29	30			

December

S	M	T	W	T	F	S
				1	2	3
4	5	6	7	8	9	10
11	12	13	14	15	16	17
18	19	20	21	22	23	24
25	26	27	28	29	30	31

JANUARY

S	M	T	W	T	F	S
1	2	3	4	5	6	7
8	9	10	11	12	13	14
15	16	17	18	19	20	21
22	23	24	25	26	27	28
29	30	31				

February

S	M	T	W	T	F	S
			1	2	3	4
5	6	7	8	9	10	11
12	13	14	15	16	17	18
19	20	21	22	23	24	25
26	27	28				

MARCH

S	M	T	W	T	F	S
			1	2	3	4
5	6	7	8	9	10	11
12	13	14	15	16	17	18
19	20	21	22	23	24	25
26	27	28	29	30	31	

April

S	M	T	W	T	F	S
						1
2	3	4	5	6	7	8
9	10	11	12	13	14	15
16	17	18	19	20	21	22
23	24	25	26	27	28	29
30						

MAY

S	M	T	W	T	F	S
	1	2	3	4	5	6
7	8	9	10	11	12	13
14	15	16	17	18	19	20
21	22	23	24	25	26	27
28	29	30	31			

June

S	M	T	W	T	F	S
				1	2	3
4	5	6	7	8	9	10
11	12	13	14	15	16	17
18	19	20	21	22	23	24
25	26	27	28	29	30	

IMPORTANT *Dates*

JULY

_____
_____
_____
_____
_____

August

_____
_____
_____
_____
_____

SEPTEMBER

_____
_____
_____
_____
_____

OCTOBER

_____
_____
_____
_____
_____

November

_____
_____
_____
_____
_____

DECEMBER

_____
_____
_____
_____
_____

JANUARY

_____
_____
_____
_____
_____

february

_____
_____
_____
_____
_____

MARCH

_____
_____
_____
_____
_____

APRIL

_____
_____
_____
_____
_____

May

_____
_____
_____
_____
_____

JUNE

_____
_____
_____
_____
_____

⚑ ★ ⚑ ★ Birthdays ★ ⚑ ★ ⚑

July	AUGUST	September

OCTOBER	November	DECEMBER

January	FEBRUARY	March

APRIL	May	JUNE

CLASS LIST

#N	FIRST NAME	LAST NAME	SEAT #	NOTES
1				
2				
3				
4				
5				
6				
7				
8				
9				
10				
11				
12				
13				
14				
15				
16				
17				
18				
19				
20				
21				
22				
23				
24				
25				
26				
27				
28				
29				
30				

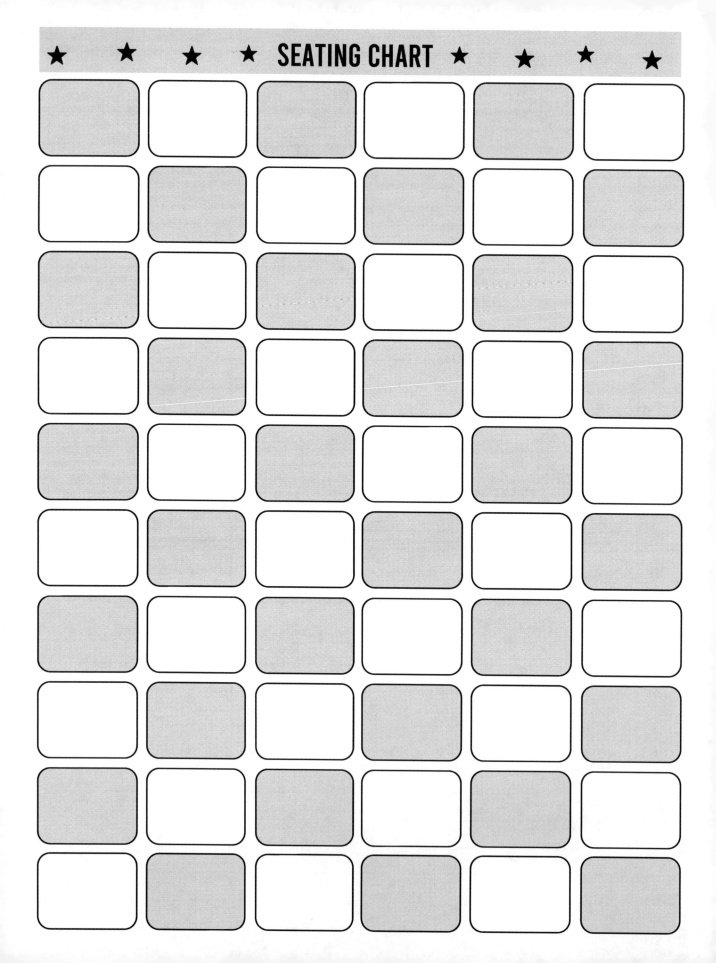

★ ★ ★ ★ SEATING CHART ★ ★ ★ ★

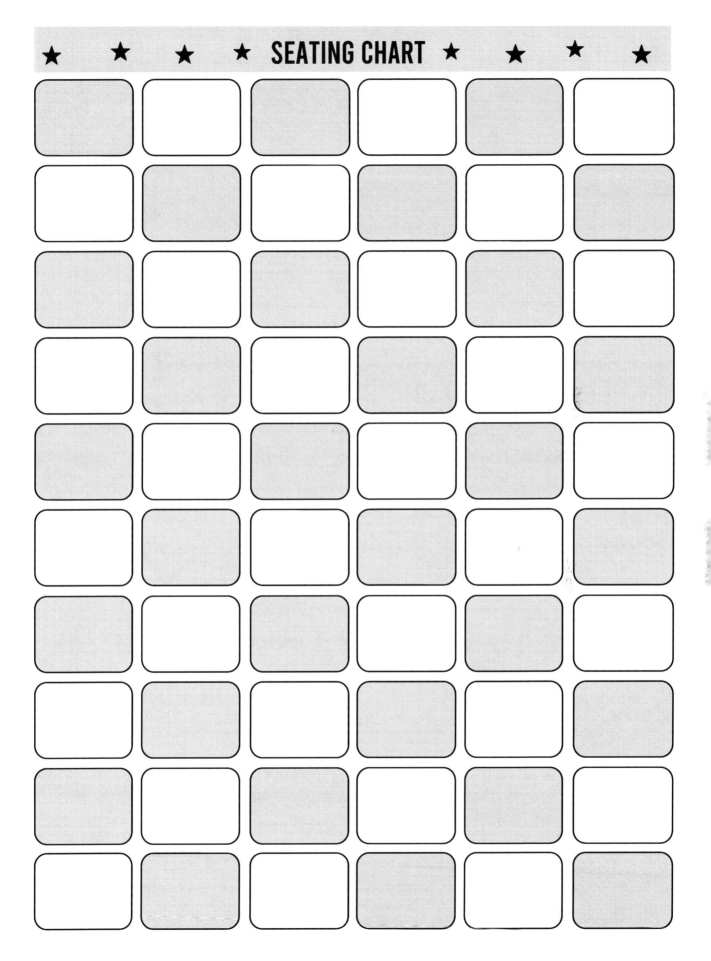

★ ★ ★ ★ SEATING CHART ★ ★ ★ ★

July

SUNDAY	MONDAY	TUESDAY	WEDNESDAY	THURSDAY
31	◯	◯	◯	◯
3	4	5	6	7
10	11	12	13	14
17	18	19	20	21
24	25	26	27	28

2022

JULY

SU	MO	TU	WE	TH	FR	SA
					1	2
3	4	5	6	7	8	9
10	11	12	13	14	15	16
17	18	19	20	21	22	23
24	25	26	27	28	29	30
31						

FRIDAY	SATURDAY
1	2
8	9
15	16
22	23
29	30

GOALS / TO DO LIST

○ _____
○ _____
○ _____
○ _____
○ _____
○ _____
○ _____
○ _____
○ _____
○ _____
○ _____

NOTES

_____
_____
_____
_____
_____
_____
_____
_____

Week of July 4th-10th

SUBJECT	MONDAY ④	TUESDAY ⑤	WEDNESDAY ⑥

THURSDAY (7)	FRIDAY (8)	SATURDAY (9)	SUNDAY (10)

GOALS / TO DO LIST

- ◯
- ◯
- ◯
- ◯
- ◯
- ◯
- ◯
- ◯
- ◯

NOTES / IDEAS

Week of July 11th-17th

SUBJECT	MONDAY ⑪	TUESDAY ⑫	WEDNESDAY ⑬

THURSDAY (14)	FRIDAY (15)	SATURDAY (16)	SUNDAY (17)

GOALS / TO DO LIST

- ○
- ○
- ○
- ○
- ○
- ○
- ○
- ○
- ○

NOTES / IDEAS

Week of July 18th-24th

SUBJECT	MONDAY ⑱	TUESDAY ⑲	WEDNESDAY ⑳

THURSDAY ㉑	FRIDAY ㉒	SATURDAY ㉓	SUNDAY ㉔

GOALS / TO DO LIST

- ○
- ○
- ○
- ○
- ○
- ○
- ○
- ○
- ○

NOTES / IDEAS

Week of July 25th-July 31st

SUBJECT	MONDAY ㉕	TUESDAY ㉖	WEDNESDAY ㉗

THURSDAY ㉘	FRIDAY ㉙	SATURDAY ㉚	SUNDAY ㉛

GOALS / TO DO LIST

- ◯
- ◯
- ◯
- ◯
- ◯
- ◯
- ◯
- ◯
- ◯

NOTES / IDEAS

ATTENDANCE Record

STUDENT	M	T	W	T	F	M	T	W	T	F	M	T	W	T	F
WEEK OF:															

A T T E N D A N C E *Record*

WEEK OF:											NOTES
STUDENT	M	T	W	T	F	M	T	W	T	F	

Grade RECORD

STUDENT	Assignment													

Grade RECORD

STUDENT	*Subject*										

NOTES

August

SUNDAY	MONDAY	TUESDAY	WEDNESDAY	THURSDAY
○	1	2	3	4
7	8	9	10	11
14	15	16	17	18
21	22	23	24	25
28	29	30	31	○

2022

FRIDAY	SATURDAY
(5)	(6)
(12)	(13)
(19)	(20)
(26)	(27)
( )	( )

AUGUST

SU	MO	TU	WE	TH	FR	SA
	1	2	3	4	5	6
7	8	9	10	11	12	13
14	15	16	17	18	19	20
21	22	23	24	25	26	27
28	29	30	31			

GOALS / TO DO LIST

○ _____
○ _____
○ _____
○ _____
○ _____
○ _____
○ _____
○ _____
○ _____
○ _____
○ _____

NOTES

Week of August 1st-7th

SUBJECT	MONDAY ①	TUESDAY ②	WEDNESDAY ③

August 2022

THURSDAY ④	FRIDAY ⑤	SATURDAY ⑥	SUNDAY ⑦

GOALS / TO DO LIST

- ○
- ○
- ○
- ○
- ○
- ○
- ○
- ○
- ○

NOTES / IDEAS

Week of August 8th-14th

SUBJECT	MONDAY (8)	TUESDAY (9)	WEDNESDAY (10)

THURSDAY (11)	FRIDAY (12)	SATURDAY (13)	SUNDAY (14)

GOALS / TO DO LIST

- ○
- ○
- ○
- ○
- ○
- ○
- ○
- ○
- ○

NOTES / IDEAS

Week of August 15th-21st

SUBJECT	MONDAY ⑮	TUESDAY ⑯	WEDNESDAY ⑰

THURSDAY ⑱	FRIDAY ⑲	SATURDAY ⑳	SUNDAY ㉑

GOALS / TO DO LIST

- ◯
- ◯
- ◯
- ◯
- ◯
- ◯
- ◯
- ◯
- ◯

NOTES / IDEAS

Week of August 22nd-28th

SUBJECT	MONDAY ㉒	TUESDAY ㉓	WEDNESDAY ㉔

THURSDAY (25)	FRIDAY (26)	SATURDAY (27)	SUNDAY (28)

GOALS / TO DO LIST

○
○
○
○
○
○
○
○
○

NOTES / IDEAS

ATTENDANCE Record

STUDENT	M	T	W	T	F	M	T	W	T	F	M	T	W	T	F
WEEK OF:															

A T T E N D A N C E *Record*

WEEK OF:											NOTES
STUDENT	M	T	W	T	F	M	T	W	T	F	

STUDENT	Assignment											

Grade RECORD

	Subject											
STUDENT												

Grade RECORD

NOTES

September

SUNDAY	MONDAY	TUESDAY	WEDNESDAY	THURSDAY
◯	◯	◯	◯	1
4	5	6	7	8
11	12	13	14	15
18	19	20	21	22
25	26	27	28	29

2022

FRIDAY	SATURDAY
(2)	(3)
(9)	(10)
(16)	(17)
(23)	(24)
(30)	( )

SEPTEMBER

SU	MO	TU	WE	TH	FR	SA
				1	2	3
4	5	6	7	8	9	10
11	12	13	14	15	16	17
18	19	20	21	22	23	24
25	26	27	28	29	30	

GOALS / TO DO LIST

- ○ _____
- ○ _____
- ○ _____
- ○ _____
- ○ _____
- ○ _____
- ○ _____
- ○ _____
- ○ _____
- ○ _____
- ○ _____

NOTES

Week of August 29th–September 4th

SUBJECT	MONDAY ㉙	TUESDAY ㉚	WEDNESDAY ㉛

September 2022

THURSDAY ①	FRIDAY ②	SATURDAY ③	SUNDAY ④

GOALS / TO DO LIST

- ◯
- ◯
- ◯
- ◯
- ◯
- ◯
- ◯
- ◯
- ◯

NOTES / IDEAS

Week of September 5th– 11th

SUBJECT	MONDAY (5)	TUESDAY (6)	WEDNESDAY (7)

THURSDAY ⑧	FRIDAY ⑨	SATURDAY ⑩	SUNDAY ⑪

GOALS / TO DO LIST

- ○
- ○
- ○
- ○
- ○
- ○
- ○
- ○
- ○

NOTES / IDEAS

Week of September 12th-18th

SUBJECT	MONDAY ⑫	TUESDAY ⑬	WEDNESDAY ⑭

THURSDAY ⑮	FRIDAY ⑯	SATURDAY ⑰	SUNDAY ⑱

GOALS / TO DO LIST

- ○
- ○
- ○
- ○
- ○
- ○
- ○
- ○
- ○

NOTES / IDEAS

Week of September 19th-25th

SUBJECT	MONDAY ⑲	TUESDAY ⑳	WEDNESDAY ㉑

THURSDAY ㉒	FRIDAY ㉓	SATURDAY ㉔	SUNDAY ㉕

GOALS / TO DO LIST

- ○
- ○
- ○
- ○
- ○
- ○
- ○
- ○
- ○

NOTES / IDEAS

SUBJECT	MONDAY ㉖	TUESDAY ㉗	WEDNESDAY ㉘

THURSDAY 29	FRIDAY 30	SATURDAY 1	SUNDAY 2

GOALS / TO DO LIST

- ◯
- ◯
- ◯
- ◯
- ◯
- ◯
- ◯
- ◯
- ◯

NOTES / IDEAS

A T T E N D A N C E *Record*

WEEK OF:															
STUDENT	M	T	W	T	F	M	T	W	T	F	M	T	W	T	F

A T T E N D A N C E *Record*

WEEK OF:											NOTES
STUDENT	M	T	W	T	F	M	T	W	T	F	

Grade RECORD		

STUDENT	*Assignment*													

Grade RECORD

STUDENT	*Subject*											

NOTES

October

SUNDAY	MONDAY	TUESDAY	WEDNESDAY	THURSDAY
30	31	◯	◯	◯
2	3	4	5	6
9	10	11	12	13
16	17	18	19	20
23	24	25	26	27

2022

FRIDAY	SATURDAY
○	①
7	8
14	15
21	22
28	29

OCTOBER

SU	MO	TU	WE	TH	FR	SA
						1
2	3	4	5	6	7	8
9	10	11	12	13	14	15
16	17	18	19	20	21	22
23	24	25	26	27	28	29
30	31					

GOALS / TO DO LIST

○ _____
○ _____
○ _____
○ _____
○ _____
○ _____
○ _____
○ _____
○ _____
○ _____
○ _____

NOTES

Week of October 3rd-9th

SUBJECT	MONDAY ③	TUESDAY ④	WEDNESDAY ⑤

THURSDAY 6	FRIDAY 7	SATURDAY 8	SUNDAY 9

GOALS / TO DO LIST

- ○
- ○
- ○
- ○
- ○
- ○
- ○
- ○
- ○

NOTES / IDEAS

Week of October 10th-16th

SUBJECT	MONDAY ⑩	TUESDAY ⑪	WEDNESDAY ⑫

THURSDAY ⑬	FRIDAY ⑭	SATURDAY ⑮	SUNDAY ⑯

GOALS / TO DO LIST

- ○
- ○
- ○
- ○
- ○
- ○
- ○
- ○
- ○

NOTES / IDEAS

Week of October 17th-23rd

SUBJECT	MONDAY ⑰	TUESDAY ⑱	WEDNESDAY ⑲

THURSDAY ⑳	FRIDAY ㉑	SATURDAY ㉒	SUNDAY ㉓

GOALS / TO DO LIST

○
○
○
○
○
○
○
○
○

NOTES / IDEAS

Week of October 24th-30th

SUBJECT	MONDAY (24)	TUESDAY (25)	WEDNESDAY (26)

THURSDAY ㉗	FRIDAY ㉘	SATURDAY ㉙	SUNDAY ㉚

GOALS / TO DO LIST

○
○
○
○
○
○
○
○
○

NOTES / IDEAS

A T T E N D A N C E *Record*

WEEK OF:															
STUDENT	M	T	W	T	F	M	T	W	T	F	M	T	W	T	F

A T T E N D A N C E *Record*

STUDENT	M	T	W	T	F	M	T	W	T	F	NOTES
WEEK OF:											

	Assignment												
STUDENT													

Grade RECORD

Grade RECORD	STUDENT	Subject												

NOTES

November

SUNDAY	MONDAY	TUESDAY	WEDNESDAY	THURSDAY
◯	◯	①	②	③
⑥	⑦	⑧	⑨	⑩
⑬	⑭	⑮	⑯	⑰
⑳	㉑	㉒	㉓	㉔
㉗	㉘	㉙	㉚	◯

2022

FRIDAY	SATURDAY
(4)	(5)
(11)	(12)
(18)	(19)
(25)	(26)
( )	( )

NOVEMBER

SU	MO	TU	WE	TH	FR	SA
		1	2	3	4	5
6	7	8	9	10	11	12
13	14	15	16	17	18	19
20	21	22	23	24	25	26
27	28	29	30			

GOALS / TO DO LIST

○ _____
○ _____
○ _____
○ _____
○ _____
○ _____
○ _____
○ _____
○ _____
○ _____
○ _____

NOTES

Week of October 31st-November 6th

SUBJECT	MONDAY 31	TUESDAY 1	WEDNESDAY 2

THURSDAY ③	FRIDAY ④	SATURDAY ⑤	SUNDAY ⑥

GOALS / TO DO LIST

- ○
- ○
- ○
- ○
- ○
- ○
- ○
- ○
- ○

NOTES / IDEAS

Week of November 7th-13th

SUBJECT	MONDAY ⑦	TUESDAY ⑧	WEDNESDAY ⑨

THURSDAY ⑩	FRIDAY ⑪	SATURDAY ⑫	SUNDAY ⑬

GOALS / TO DO LIST

- ○
- ○
- ○
- ○
- ○
- ○
- ○
- ○
- ○

NOTES / IDEAS

Week of November 14th-20th

SUBJECT	MONDAY (14)	TUESDAY (15)	WEDNESDAY (16)

THURSDAY ⑰	FRIDAY ⑱	SATURDAY ⑲	SUNDAY ⑳

GOALS / TO DO LIST

- ○
- ○
- ○
- ○
- ○
- ○
- ○
- ○
- ○

NOTES / IDEAS

Week of November 21st-27th

SUBJECT	MONDAY 21	TUESDAY 22	WEDNESDAY 23

THURSDAY (24)	FRIDAY (25)	SATURDAY (26)	SUNDAY (27)

GOALS / TO DO LIST

- ○
- ○
- ○
- ○
- ○
- ○
- ○
- ○
- ○

NOTES / IDEAS

A T T E N D A N C E *Record*

WEEK OF:															
STUDENT	M	T	W	T	F	M	T	W	T	F	M	T	W	T	F

A T T E N D A N C E *Record*

STUDENT	M	T	W	T	F	M	T	W	T	F	NOTES
WEEK OF:											

STUDENT	Assignment														

Grade RECORD

STUDENT	*Subject*												

Grade RECORD

NOTES

December

SUNDAY	MONDAY	TUESDAY	WEDNESDAY	THURSDAY
◯	◯	◯	◯	1
4	5	6	7	8
11	12	13	14	15
18	19	20	21	22
25	26	27	28	29

2022

DECEMBER

SU	MO	TU	WE	TH	FR	SA
				1	2	3
4	5	6	7	8	9	10
11	12	13	14	15	16	17
18	19	20	21	22	23	24
25	26	27	28	29	30	31

FRIDAY	SATURDAY
(2)	(3)
(9)	(10)
(16)	(17)
(23)	(24)
(30)	(31)

GOALS / TO DO LIST

○ _____
○ _____
○ _____
○ _____
○ _____
○ _____
○ _____
○ _____
○ _____
○ _____
○ _____

NOTES

_____
_____
_____
_____
_____
_____
_____
_____
_____

Week of November 28th-December 4th

SUBJECT	MONDAY (28)	TUESDAY (29)	WEDNESDAY (30)

THURSDAY ①	FRIDAY ②	SATURDAY ③	SUNDAY ④

GOALS / TO DO LIST

○
○
○
○
○
○
○
○
○

NOTES / IDEAS

Week of December 5th-11th

SUBJECT	MONDAY ⑤	TUESDAY ⑥	WEDNESDAY ⑦

THURSDAY (8)	FRIDAY (9)	SATURDAY (10)	SUNDAY (11)

GOALS / TO DO LIST

- ○
- ○
- ○
- ○
- ○
- ○
- ○
- ○
- ○

NOTES / IDEAS

Week of December 12th-18th

SUBJECT	MONDAY ⑫	TUESDAY ⑬	WEDNESDAY ⑭

THURSDAY ⑮	FRIDAY ⑯	SATURDAY ⑰	SUNDAY ⑱

GOALS / TO DO LIST

- ○
- ○
- ○
- ○
- ○
- ○
- ○
- ○
- ○

NOTES / IDEAS

Week of December 19th-25th

SUBJECT	MONDAY ⑲	TUESDAY ⑳	WEDNESDAY ㉑

THURSDAY ㉒	FRIDAY ㉓	SATURDAY ㉔	SUNDAY ㉕

GOALS / TO DO LIST

- ○
- ○
- ○
- ○
- ○
- ○
- ○
- ○
- ○

NOTES / IDEAS

Week of December 26th-January 1st

SUBJECT	MONDAY ㉖	TUESDAY ㉗	WEDNESDAY ㉘

THURSDAY 29	FRIDAY 30	SATURDAY 31	SUNDAY 1

GOALS / TO DO LIST

- ◯
- ◯
- ◯
- ◯
- ◯
- ◯
- ◯
- ◯
- ◯

NOTES / IDEAS

A T T E N D A N C E *Record*

STUDENT	M	T	W	T	F	M	T	W	T	F	M	T	W	T	F
WEEK OF:															

A T T E N D A N C E *Record*

STUDENT	M	T	W	T	F	M	T	W	T	F	NOTES
WEEK OF:											

Grade RECORD

STUDENT	*Assignment*													

STUDENT	Subject											

Grade RECORD

NOTES

January

SUNDAY	MONDAY	TUESDAY	WEDNESDAY	THURSDAY
1	2	3	4	5
8	9	10	11	12
15	16	17	18	19
22	23	24	25	26
29	30	31		

2023

FRIDAY	SATURDAY
(6)	(7)
(13)	(14)
(20)	(21)
(27)	(28)
( )	( )

JANUARY

SU	MO	TU	WE	TH	FR	SA
1	2	3	4	5	6	7
8	9	10	11	12	13	14
15	16	17	18	19	20	21
22	23	24	25	26	27	28
29	30	31				

GOALS / TO DO LIST

○ _____
○ _____
○ _____
○ _____
○ _____
○ _____
○ _____
○ _____
○ _____
○ _____
○ _____

NOTES

Week of January 2nd-8th

SUBJECT	MONDAY ②	TUESDAY ③	WEDNESDAY ④

THURSDAY ⑤	FRIDAY ⑥	SATURDAY ⑦	SUNDAY ⑧

GOALS / TO DO LIST

- ○
- ○
- ○
- ○
- ○
- ○
- ○
- ○
- ○

NOTES / IDEAS

Week of January 9th–15th

SUBJECT	MONDAY ⑨	TUESDAY ⑩	WEDNESDAY ⑪

January 2023

THURSDAY ⑫	FRIDAY ⑬	SATURDAY ⑭	SUNDAY ⑮

GOALS / TO DO LIST

- ◯
- ◯
- ◯
- ◯
- ◯
- ◯
- ◯
- ◯
- ◯

NOTES / IDEAS

Week of January 16th-22nd

SUBJECT	MONDAY (16)	TUESDAY (17)	WEDNESDAY (18)

THURSDAY 19	FRIDAY 20	SATURDAY 21	SUNDAY 22

GOALS / TO DO LIST

- ○
- ○
- ○
- ○
- ○
- ○
- ○
- ○
- ○

NOTES / IDEAS

Week of January 23rd-29th

SUBJECT	MONDAY ㉓	TUESDAY ㉔	WEDNESDAY ㉕

THURSDAY (26)	FRIDAY (27)	SATURDAY (28)	SUNDAY (29)

GOALS / TO DO LIST

- ○
- ○
- ○
- ○
- ○
- ○
- ○
- ○
- ○

NOTES / IDEAS

ATTENDANCE Record

STUDENT	M	T	W	T	F	M	T	W	T	F	M	T	W	T	F
WEEK OF:															

ATTENDANCE Record

WEEK OF:											NOTES
STUDENT	M	T	W	T	F	M	T	W	T	F	

STUDENT	*Assignment*												

G r a d e R E C O R D

STUDENT	*subject*														

Grade *RECORD*

NOTES

february

SUNDAY	MONDAY	TUESDAY	WEDNESDAY	THURSDAY
◯	◯	◯	1	2
5	6	7	8	9
12	13	14	15	16
19	20	21	22	23
26	27	28	◯	◯

2023

FRIDAY	SATURDAY
(3)	(4)
(10)	(11)
(17)	(18)
(24)	(25)
◯	◯

FEBRUARY

SU	MO	TU	WE	TH	FR	SA
			1	2	3	4
5	6	7	8	9	10	11
12	13	14	15	16	17	18
19	20	21	22	23	24	25
26	27	28				

GOALS / TO DO LIST

◯ _____
◯ _____
◯ _____
◯ _____
◯ _____
◯ _____
◯ _____
◯ _____
◯ _____
◯ _____
◯ _____

NOTES

Week of January 30th–February 5th

SUBJECT	MONDAY 30	TUESDAY 31	WEDNESDAY 1

THURSDAY ②	FRIDAY ③	SATURDAY ④	SUNDAY ⑤

GOALS / TO DO LIST

- ○
- ○
- ○
- ○
- ○
- ○
- ○
- ○
- ○

NOTES / IDEAS

Week of February 6th-12th

SUBJECT	MONDAY ⑥	TUESDAY ⑦	WEDNESDAY ⑧

THURSDAY 9	FRIDAY 10	SATURDAY 11	SUNDAY 12

GOALS / TO DO LIST

- ○
- ○
- ○
- ○
- ○
- ○
- ○
- ○
- ○

NOTES / IDEAS

Week of february 13th-19th

SUBJECT	MONDAY ⑬	TUESDAY ⑭	WEDNESDAY ⑮

THURSDAY ⑯	FRIDAY ⑰	SATURDAY ⑱	SUNDAY ⑲

GOALS / TO DO LIST

- ○
- ○
- ○
- ○
- ○
- ○
- ○
- ○
- ○

NOTES / IDEAS

Week of February 20th-26th

SUBJECT	MONDAY 20	TUESDAY 21	WEDNESDAY 22

THURSDAY ㉓	FRIDAY ㉔	SATURDAY ㉕	SUNDAY ㉖

GOALS / TO DO LIST

- ◯
- ◯
- ◯
- ◯
- ◯
- ◯
- ◯
- ◯
- ◯

NOTES / IDEAS

A T T E N D A N C E *Record*

STUDENT	M	T	W	T	F	M	T	W	T	F	M	T	W	T	F
WEEK OF:															

ATTENDANCE Record

WEEK OF:											NOTES
STUDENT	M	T	W	T	F	M	T	W	T	F	

	Assignment													
STUDENT														

Grade Record

Grade RECORD

STUDENT	*Subject*													

NOTES

March

SUNDAY	MONDAY	TUESDAY	WEDNESDAY	THURSDAY
◯	◯	◯	1	2
5	6	7	8	9
12	13	14	15	16
19	20	21	22	23
26	27	28	29	30

2023

FRIDAY	SATURDAY
③	④
⑩	⑪
⑰	⑱
㉔	㉕
㉛	○

MARCH

SU	MO	TU	WE	TH	FR	SA
			1	2	3	4
5	6	7	8	9	10	11
12	13	14	15	16	17	18
19	20	21	22	23	24	25
26	27	28	29	30	31	

GOALS / TO DO LIST

○ _____
○ _____
○ _____
○ _____
○ _____
○ _____
○ _____
○ _____
○ _____
○ _____
○ _____

NOTES

Week of February 27th-March 5th

SUBJECT	MONDAY (27)	TUESDAY (28)	WEDNESDAY (1)

THURSDAY ②	FRIDAY ③	SATURDAY ④	SUNDAY ⑤

GOALS / TO DO LIST

- ○
- ○
- ○
- ○
- ○
- ○
- ○
- ○
- ○

NOTES / IDEAS

Week of March 6th-12th

SUBJECT	MONDAY ⑥	TUESDAY ⑦	WEDNESDAY ⑧

THURSDAY ⑨	FRIDAY ⑩	SATURDAY ⑪	SUNDAY ⑫

GOALS / TO DO LIST

- ◯
- ◯
- ◯
- ◯
- ◯
- ◯
- ◯
- ◯
- ◯

NOTES / IDEAS

Week of March 13th-19th

SUBJECT	MONDAY ⑬	TUESDAY ⑭	WEDNESDAY ⑮

THURSDAY ⑯	FRIDAY ⑰	SATURDAY ⑱	SUNDAY ⑲

GOALS / TO DO LIST

- ◯
- ◯
- ◯
- ◯
- ◯
- ◯
- ◯
- ◯
- ◯

NOTES / IDEAS

Week of March 20th-26th

SUBJECT	MONDAY 20	TUESDAY 21	WEDNESDAY 22

THURSDAY ㉓	FRIDAY ㉔	SATURDAY ㉕	SUNDAY ㉖

GOALS / TO DO LIST

- ○
- ○
- ○
- ○
- ○
- ○
- ○
- ○
- ○

NOTES / IDEAS

Week of March 27th-April 2nd

SUBJECT	MONDAY (27)	TUESDAY (28)	WEDNESDAY (29)

THURSDAY ㉚	FRIDAY ㉛	SATURDAY ①	SUNDAY ②

GOALS / TO DO LIST

- ○
- ○
- ○
- ○
- ○
- ○
- ○
- ○
- ○

NOTES / IDEAS

ATTENDANCE Record

WEEK OF:															
STUDENT	M	T	W	T	F	M	T	W	T	F	M	T	W	T	F

A T T E N D A N C E *Record*

WEEK OF:											NOTES
STUDENT	M	T	W	T	F	M	T	W	T	F	

Grade RECORD

STUDENT	Assignment												

Grade RECORD

STUDENT	*Subject*															

NOTES

April

SUNDAY	MONDAY	TUESDAY	WEDNESDAY	THURSDAY
30	○	○	○	○
2	3	4	5	6
9	10	11	12	13
16	17	18	19	20
23	24	25	26	27

2023

FRIDAY	SATURDAY
◯	①
⑦	⑧
⑭	⑮
㉑	㉒
㉘	㉙

APRIL

SU	MO	TU	WE	TH	FR	SA
						1
2	3	4	5	6	7	8
9	10	11	12	13	14	15
16	17	18	19	20	21	22
23	24	25	26	27	28	29
30						

GOALS / TO DO LIST

- ◯ _____
- ◯ _____
- ◯ _____
- ◯ _____
- ◯ _____
- ◯ _____
- ◯ _____
- ◯ _____
- ◯ _____
- ◯ _____
- ◯ _____

NOTES

Week of April 3rd–9th

SUBJECT	MONDAY ③	TUESDAY ④	WEDNESDAY ⑤

THURSDAY (6)	FRIDAY (7)	SATURDAY (8)	SUNDAY (9)

GOALS / TO DO LIST

- ○
- ○
- ○
- ○
- ○
- ○
- ○
- ○
- ○

NOTES / IDEAS

Week of April 10th-16th

SUBJECT	MONDAY 10	TUESDAY 11	WEDNESDAY 12

THURSDAY 13	FRIDAY 14	SATURDAY 15	SUNDAY 16

GOALS / TO DO LIST

- ○
- ○
- ○
- ○
- ○
- ○
- ○
- ○
- ○

NOTES / IDEAS

Week of April 17th-23rd

SUBJECT	MONDAY ⑰	TUESDAY ⑱	WEDNESDAY ⑲

April 2023

THURSDAY 20	FRIDAY 21	SATURDAY 22	SUNDAY 23

GOALS / TO DO LIST

- ◯
- ◯
- ◯
- ◯
- ◯
- ◯
- ◯
- ◯
- ◯

NOTES / IDEAS

Week of April 24th-30th

SUBJECT	MONDAY ㉔	TUESDAY ㉕	WEDNESDAY ㉖

THURSDAY ㉗	FRIDAY ㉘	SATURDAY ㉙	SUNDAY ㉚

GOALS / TO DO LIST

- ◯
- ◯
- ◯
- ◯
- ◯
- ◯
- ◯
- ◯
- ◯

NOTES / IDEAS

A T T E N D A N C E *Record*

STUDENT	M	T	W	T	F	M	T	W	T	F	M	T	W	T	F
WEEK OF:															

A T T E N D A N C E *Record*

WEEK OF:											NOTES
STUDENT	M	T	W	T	F	M	T	W	T	F	

STUDENT	Assignment													

Grade RECORD

Grade RECORD

STUDENT	*Subject*									

NOTES

May

SUNDAY	MONDAY	TUESDAY	WEDNESDAY	THURSDAY
○	1	2	3	4
7	8	9	10	11
14	15	16	17	18
21	22	23	24	25
28	29	30	31	○

2023

FRIDAY	SATURDAY
(5)	(6)
(12)	(13)
(19)	(20)
(26)	(27)
○	○

MAY

SU	MO	TU	WE	TH	FR	SA
	1	2	3	4	5	6
7	8	9	10	11	12	13
14	15	16	17	18	19	20
21	22	23	24	25	26	27
28	29	30	31			

GOALS / TO DO LIST

○ _____
○ _____
○ _____
○ _____
○ _____
○ _____
○ _____
○ _____
○ _____
○ _____
○ _____

NOTES

Week of May 1st-7th

SUBJECT	MONDAY ①	TUESDAY ②	WEDNESDAY ③

THURSDAY ④	FRIDAY ⑤	SATURDAY ⑥	SUNDAY ⑦

GOALS / TO DO LIST

- ○
- ○
- ○
- ○
- ○
- ○
- ○
- ○
- ○

NOTES / IDEAS

Week of May 8th-14th

SUBJECT	MONDAY (8)	TUESDAY (9)	WEDNESDAY (10)

THURSDAY (11)	FRIDAY (12)	SATURDAY (13)	SUNDAY (14)

GOALS / TO DO LIST

- ○
- ○
- ○
- ○
- ○
- ○
- ○
- ○
- ○

NOTES / IDEAS

Week of May 15th-21st

SUBJECT	MONDAY (15)	TUESDAY (16)	WEDNESDAY (17)

May 2023

THURSDAY ⑱	FRIDAY ⑲	SATURDAY ⑳	SUNDAY ㉑

GOALS / TO DO LIST

○
○
○
○
○
○
○
○
○

NOTES / IDEAS

Week of May 22nd-28th

SUBJECT	MONDAY ㉒	TUESDAY ㉓	WEDNESDAY ㉔

THURSDAY ㉕	FRIDAY ㉖	SATURDAY ㉗	SUNDAY ㉘

GOALS / TO DO LIST

- ○
- ○
- ○
- ○
- ○
- ○
- ○
- ○
- ○

NOTES / IDEAS

A T T E N D A N C E *Record*

WEEK OF:															
STUDENT	M	T	W	T	F	M	T	W	T	F	M	T	W	T	F

A T T E N D A N C E *Record*

WEEK OF:											NOTES
STUDENT	M	T	W	T	F	M	T	W	T	F	

STUDENT	Assignment														

Grade RECORD

STUDENT	*Subject*											

Grade Record

NOTES

June

SUNDAY	MONDAY	TUESDAY	WEDNESDAY	THURSDAY
◯	◯	◯	◯	1
4	5	6	7	8
11	12	13	14	15
18	19	20	21	22
25	26	27	28	29

2023

SU	MO	TU	WE	TH	FR	SA
				1	2	3
4	5	6	7	8	9	10
11	12	13	14	15	16	17
18	19	20	21	22	23	24
25	26	27	28	29	30	

FRIDAY	SATURDAY
2	**3**
9	**10**
16	**17**
23	**24**
30	

GOALS / TO DO LIST

○ _____
○ _____
○ _____
○ _____
○ _____
○ _____
○ _____
○ _____
○ _____
○ _____
○ _____

NOTES

Week of May 29th-June 4th

SUBJECT	MONDAY ㉙	TUESDAY ㉚	WEDNESDAY ㉛

THURSDAY ①	FRIDAY ②	SATURDAY ③	SUNDAY ④

GOALS / TO DO LIST

- ○
- ○
- ○
- ○
- ○
- ○
- ○
- ○
- ○

NOTES / IDEAS

Week of June 5th-11th

SUBJECT	MONDAY ⑤	TUESDAY ⑥	WEDNESDAY ⑦

THURSDAY ⑧	FRIDAY ⑨	SATURDAY ⑩	SUNDAY ⑪

GOALS / TO DO LIST

- ○
- ○
- ○
- ○
- ○
- ○
- ○
- ○
- ○

NOTES / IDEAS

Week of June 12th-18th

SUBJECT	MONDAY ⑫	TUESDAY ⑬	WEDNESDAY ⑭

THURSDAY ⑮	FRIDAY ⑯	SATURDAY ⑰	SUNDAY ⑱

GOALS / TO DO LIST

- ○
- ○
- ○
- ○
- ○
- ○
- ○
- ○
- ○

NOTES / IDEAS

Week of June 19th-25th

SUBJECT	MONDAY ⑲	TUESDAY ⑳	WEDNESDAY ㉑

June 2023

THURSDAY (22)	FRIDAY (23)	SATURDAY (24)	SUNDAY (25)

GOALS / TO DO LIST

- ◯
- ◯
- ◯
- ◯
- ◯
- ◯
- ◯
- ◯
- ◯

NOTES / IDEAS

Week of June 26th-July 2nd

SUBJECT	MONDAY 26	TUESDAY 27	WEDNESDAY 28

THURSDAY ㉙	FRIDAY ㉚	SATURDAY ①	SUNDAY ②

GOALS / TO DO LIST

- ○
- ○
- ○
- ○
- ○
- ○
- ○
- ○
- ○

NOTES / IDEAS

A T T E N D A N C E *Record*

STUDENT	M	T	W	T	F	M	T	W	T	F	M	T	W	T	F
WEEK OF:															

ATTENDANCE Record

STUDENT	M	T	W	T	F	M	T	W	T	F	NOTES
WEEK OF:											

Grade RECORD		

Grade RECORD

STUDENT	*Assignment*											

Grade RECORD

STUDENT	*Subject*													

NOTES

PARENTS CONTACT

STUDENT:_____

PARENTS:_____

PHONE:_____

E-MAIL:_____

NOTES:_____

STUDENT:_____

PARENTS:_____

PHONE:_____

E-MAIL:_____

NOTES:_____

STUDENT:_____

PARENTS:_____

PHONE:_____

E-MAIL:_____

NOTES:_____

STUDENT:_____

PARENTS:_____

PHONE:_____

E-MAIL:_____

NOTES:_____

STUDENT:_____

PARENTS:_____

PHONE:_____

E-MAIL:_____

NOTES:_____

STUDENT:_____

PARENTS:_____

PHONE:_____

E-MAIL:_____

NOTES:_____

STUDENT:_____

PARENTS:_____

PHONE:_____

E-MAIL:_____

NOTES:_____

STUDENT:_____

PARENTS:_____

PHONE:_____

E-MAIL:_____

NOTES:_____

STUDENT:_____

PARENTS:_____

PHONE:_____

E-MAIL:_____

NOTES:_____

STUDENT:_____

PARENTS:_____

PHONE:_____

E-MAIL:_____

NOTES:_____

PARENTS CONTACT

STUDENT:_____

PARENTS:_____

PHONE:_____

E-MAIL:_____

NOTES:_____

STUDENT:_____

PARENTS:_____

PHONE:_____

E-MAIL:_____

NOTES:_____

STUDENT:_____

PARENTS:_____

PHONE:_____

E-MAIL:_____

NOTES:_____

STUDENT:_____

PARENTS:_____

PHONE:_____

E-MAIL:_____

NOTES:_____

STUDENT:_____

PARENTS:_____

PHONE:_____

E-MAIL:_____

NOTES:_____

STUDENT:_____

PARENTS:_____

PHONE:_____

E-MAIL:_____

NOTES:_____

STUDENT:_____

PARENTS:_____

PHONE:_____

E-MAIL:_____

NOTES:_____

STUDENT:_____

PARENTS:_____

PHONE:_____

E-MAIL:_____

NOTES:_____

STUDENT:_____

PARENTS:_____

PHONE:_____

E-MAIL:_____

NOTES:_____

STUDENT:_____

PARENTS:_____

PHONE:_____

E-MAIL:_____

NOTES:_____

PARENTS CONTACT

STUDENT:_____

PARENTS:_____

PHONE:_____

E-MAIL:_____

NOTES:_____

STUDENT:_____

PARENTS:_____

PHONE:_____

E-MAIL:_____

NOTES:_____

STUDENT:_____

PARENTS:_____

PHONE:_____

E-MAIL:_____

NOTES:_____

STUDENT:_____

PARENTS:_____

PHONE:_____

E-MAIL:_____

NOTES:_____

STUDENT:_____

PARENTS:_____

PHONE:_____

E-MAIL:_____

NOTES:_____

STUDENT:_____

PARENTS:_____

PHONE:_____

E-MAIL:_____

NOTES:_____

STUDENT:_____

PARENTS:_____

PHONE:_____

E-MAIL:_____

NOTES:_____

STUDENT:_____

PARENTS:_____

PHONE:_____

E-MAIL:_____

NOTES:_____

STUDENT:_____

PARENTS:_____

PHONE:_____

E-MAIL:_____

NOTES:_____

STUDENT:_____

PARENTS:_____

PHONE:_____

E-MAIL:_____

NOTES:_____

Made in the USA
Las Vegas, NV
19 August 2022